FORGED LIGHT

Forged Light

POEMS BY MARGARET LLOYD

ACKNOWLEDGMENTS

Poems in this book first appeared in the following journals and anthologies, sometimes in earlier versions. Grateful acknowledgment is given to these publications.

The American Voice: "The Bay Window," "Second World"
The Comstock Review: "The Sweater"
The Gettysburg Review: "Driving Through a World Not Seen," "Not About Daily Life"
The Loft Anthology: *New England Poetry and Art*: "Ariadne"
Measure: "In the Presence of the Lord," "Marriage"
Open Field: *Poems from Group 18*: "Discordia"
Other Land: *Contemporary Poems on Wales and Welsh-American Experience*: "Crossing"
Planet: *The Welsh Internationalist*: "Early Happiness," "A World Wanting a Voice," "Finally,"
      "West Kennet Long Barrow," "Untitled"
Theodate: *The Poetry Journal of Hill-Stead Museum*: "Annunciation," "Eternity," "Instruction"
Poetry East: "Magdalen," "Rembrandt's Women," "The Demand," "Night Watch"
Poetry Wales: "City and Lake"
Willow Springs: "Red Dress" (Winner of the Vachel Lindsay Poetry Award)

Thanks are due to the Corporation of Yaddo for granting a residency during which a number of the poems in *Forged Light* found their first form and to Springfield College for the gift of sabbatical time.

The epigram from the *Book of Taliesin* is translated by Marged Haycock in *Legendary Poems from the Book of Taliesin* (Aberystwyth: CMCS, 2007).

The epigram to Part IV is a translation of a Latin verse lament found in *Y Cynfeirdd Cymreig*, National Library of Wales, Peniarth MS 201.

ISBN: 978-0-9831471-1-4
LIBRARY OF CONGRESS NUMBER: 2013912726

Set in Arno Pro types
Printed and bound by Collective Copies, Inc.

Open Field Press
126 Main Street
Northampton, MA 01060
www.openfieldpress.com

Er cof am fy mam, gyda chariad
MAIR ELVIRA LLOYD
In memory of my mother, with love

Contents

Why is a stone so heavy?
why is a thorn-bush so sharp?
Do you know which is better—
its base or its tip?
What made a partition
between man and the cold?
Whose death is better:
a young person or an old one?
Do you know what you are
when you are asleep:
a body or a soul
or a pale mysterious thing?
O skillful one of song,
why don't you tell me?

From the *Book of Taliesin*
(Welsh, 14th century)

I · TALES

Discordia

The goddess of discord is always just beyond our sight,
behind the hedge with her toes gripping the dirt.
She strains to watch the company and listens to the laughter.
Only she knows what is about to happen.

The day is almost perfect with the light shining
on one side of the beeches and the shadows
lifting the sun. The low hum of crickets
barely suggesting the cold to come.

There is never an invitation for her, but what would we do
without her? Without the apple she tosses into our midst
whenever the earth is about to seem like heaven. What would we do
without the launching of the fast ships over the black sea,

followed by slaughter and then the journey home?
Without tales that people later tell around the embers,
beguiling long hours of darkness,
looking at the high stars, the harp singing.

The Surrender of Thetis

Finally how easily she lay on her back for him.
How quickly in that field somewhere close to the river.
She wore a blue bathing suit thinking
isn't that what women wore on a summer's day on earth.
They lay on an old blanket, the sky protecting them
and a stand of apple trees, a field of tall corn.
On the path the tractors made, they entered each other,
pretending that in this world they had a place.
The long geese had not yet begun to fly south.
Men were walking along the side of the highway
carrying yellow bags, collecting litter in the afternoon's heat.

The Demand

He is looking at fourteen wild turkeys in the apple grove
on the morning she knows she has to give him up.
The turkeys are feeding on the ground covered with snow
and it will soon rain. In her yard, other birds are feeding—
goldfinch, the slate-colored juncos, starlings.
They, too, know something about the weather,
how it shifts suddenly, its icy harshness.

Is this how Calypso felt in her hollow cave?
Seven years seems like a long time, but to her it was nothing;
there was all of time still to come. Calypso, shuddering,
gave Odysseus tools and the wood to make a boat.
The demand was not only to let him go, but to provide
the means to go—the raft of trees that carried him
over the broad back of the sea towards home.

Ariadne

Not a sail in sight, not a trace of the ship's path
through the blue of the Aegean morning. Only

a distant landscape suggesting there are other
destinations in the world. One hand goes to her head,

holding the cloud of her confusion; the other
outstretched, almost waving, almost beckoning,

but finally as if to say *stop, wait. Come back.*
She saved him, he would remember her,

and she knows how memorable she is,
her bright body circling his in the night.

But the world is relentless and says everything,
presenting now its blank backside.

The water lapping at her feet, almost whispering,
this is all now. It is your fate not to be remembered.

Persephone Delivered

And when I was gone
a long time and no one
came looking for me,
and then no one cared when
I came home, I knew
I was out in the world alone.
The sky was forever
and so was the night.
No thread holding me here—
only threads I made up
to keep me feeling
safe—to have an excuse
not to let anyone penetrate
my heart or my skin.
Even my dreams I kept
clean so there was nothing
to stir desire. And truly,
it was all my own doing.
Until a god bent down
his head towards me
and said *enough*.
Enough. It was then
I picked myself up
and walked into hell
and back again, into
hell and back again.
I was by myself, but
somehow I didn't
care anymore, flung
as I was, into the mortal
and immortal world.

Annunciation

Three angels sit at a table turning pots,
discussing the possibility of his birth.
Tools lie on the table in front of them.
As the clay spins, the angel in the middle
places a finger in the center to help it rise.
After it has been decided, the one with the red scarf
appears to the woman with the news:
no ordinary happiness for her—
no looking with simple pleasure out the window
at the lupine, wild carrot, and mustard.
The angel's feet don't quite reach the ground.
He returns to the clay, failing sometimes,
and sometimes making a pot so shapely and thin,
it leaps like the gazelle he once saw
in early spring on earth.

Magdalen

I am taking everything off—my lipstick,
lotion, my perfume—and I'm washing
my face and letting you watch as I do this.

Nothing is going to happen, but I will be clean.
Look at me as it all comes off.

In the middle of doing this, I can see
you are already leaving me. I want you to stay

until I am down to the bone.
I don't think you will.

Christ left his linen cloths in the tomb,
and I found them.

But I know you will not come back to see
my soft clothes folded in the corner of the room.

Raised

I was in the boat in the storm,
one of the disciples. Not the one
with his leg over the side,
rushing towards love. Not anymore.
I was eyeing the high waves, worrying
about our net full of fish. I was also aware
of the dead man standing
where the waves touched the shore.
Afterwards I know I will tell the story,
how afraid I was, how unsure,
looking both ways and signaling.

In David's City

Bathsheba sat a long time with the letter
from King David in her hand.
Her maidservant washed her feet and dried her back.
She braided and beaded her red hair
while the great masters painted her over and over.

Still Bathsheba sat thinking, abandon me.
Do not look at me anymore. Leave me
to stones and the edges of the world,
to the spume of waves on ragged rocks,
to fish in the shoals and the wild cactus.
I am tired of the vaulted sky and the frame of the world.

Sebastian

My eyes have nowhere to look,
banished, as I am, from duration.

Each taut arrow goes into a different part
of my astounded body, which has toiled so long.

A white cloth winds around my life.
I am ashamed, I tell you. I am ashamed

there was no joy for me. No comfort.
No large or small encounter with God,

as some might think. But there was
a demand—the call of a bird

beyond the clamor of blood.
The scud of yellow sky before the night.

Light shining on the backs of the dead.
Now only arrows pierce my shoulder,

knee, gut, thigh. My heart.
There was no choice but to live this way,

and I'll die another way. Perhaps
thrown into the sewer.

And is this not a life?
There are lives like this.

Brontë

He was the main player in their childhood
kingdoms and trysts, intrigues
of a secret world, furiously
writing scripts in a miniature hand.
All Branwell finally wanted was a little god
and an accepted friend. Evenings
he drank in Haworth's one tavern
while his famous sisters wrote.
In the stairwell hung his portrait of the four,
his own visage later blacked out.
Some of us excuse ourselves,
choose one life over another—in his case
a life of secrecy and anonymity
with, I imagine, its own purposes.
As the wind swept over the moors,
through the stiff grasses and harebells,
the four sat by the parsonage fire,
completing their separate assignments.

Rhiannon Speaks

I have arrived to ask you,
can you imagine there is
some relief from leaving
being human and becoming
what runs in the fields
or sleeps in the stable,
what eats grasses and carries
the burdens of the world?
It is a relief, I tell you,
the way shame releases us
from grandiosity, from showing
only pride. Let those who want
to take things away from you
have their way. Let people
who wish to save themselves
by using you, save themselves.
The truth is I became more
than human, not less,
when I became the horse,
carrying others on my back.

Greek Fragment

In the ancient Agora a bell rings.
A little girl with bronze bracelets
on each wrist, a ring on her left hand,
died 3000 years ago. We can see
the long pin that fastened the garment
around her small shoulders.
She lies on her back—her grave
protected for centuries by fieldstones.
There is nothing to do
but to live now and speak,
holding my shoulders back,
straightening my spine
to honor myself and that small girl.
And perhaps to honor some god.

II · WORLD WANTING A VOICE

Crossing

The mist is a line of ghosts drifting
westward over the still water.
I dream this lake is the ocean we crossed
from Liverpool to New York harbor.
I was two years old, at sea for eight days.
We arrived with thirteen trunks,
a one-ton crate of furniture.
People in my family have died and are still
dying across the ocean. So many ghosts
between me and the far shore.
Water laps against the rowboat.
I turn and see the lilies are open.
This is America. This is the state of Maine.
Everyday I memorize details:
Yarrow is the brightest flower before the dark comes.
When the crows stop screaming,
small birds can be heard.
I remember the furniture that came with us:
a carved oak sideboard and dining room table,
granddaughter clock with two chimes,
glass-fronted bookcases.
Another country and another
language lived in our house.
I now can see to the other side,
but can't penetrate the stand of trees.
The mist is lifting, but the ghosts still drift.
This is the somewhere else I have always been.

Early Happiness

I think of our beginnings
under the slanted attic ceiling.
Outside our window
the eighteenth-century church
with its graveyard and beyond that
the medieval castle ruins, the sea
with the Ystwyth flowing into it.
Then the second room of our marriage
where we did all of our living,
day and night, in the basement
of a Victorian house in Yorkshire
where the servants once lived.
A grandfather clock against the wall
at the foot of our bed.
Next door, the narrow kitchen
with large hooks in the ceiling
where they used to hang meat.
The immense, polluted, industrial
city of Leeds spread from our
front door. Across the street
the communal gardens, roses
and brussel sprouts blooming in winter.
Milk every morning in glass bottles
standing in our back garden near the shed,
the cream stolen early by birds.

Driving Through a World Not Seen

The narrow road winds between sea and mountain.
You point out a derelict stone house almost hidden
by wild fuchsia and a cow. Sometimes a world

is not seen until someone speaks.
The way Naoise did not recognize Deirdre
until she bound him with her voice. And then we're told

the story of their wanderings and their love.
Broad-winged hawks swoop over us as we travel
away from the coast where we lived for a while.

Every day walking on the beach we could see
where the tide reached the night before
by the jagged lines of seaweed on the sands.

We're driving north in midsummer
when only the tips of foxgloves bloom,
a color close to blood.

A World Wanting a Voice

I wore white. Their winter boots were muddy,
but I took the children in my arms to climb
the hill home because they were tired. Three

bodies moving together like one hymn
sung slowly by a small congregation.
That was years ago in late spring.

Farmers were planting corn while the sun shone,
but out of the far corner of my eye
the magnolia blossoms looked like snow,

a snow that later fell out of the sky,
dumb and cold. Absolute in its demand.
Blinding me on that same hill where I

had struggled with the children's weight, my mind
intent on home. A world wanting a voice.
Wanting hours, days, years; the passage of time

measured by the passing of nights, close
to words and the shifting moon. Wanting to bind
hands and eyes, to take away any choice

and send me singing into the snow, blind
and failing, leaving the first world behind.

West Kennet Long Barrow

A cow rubs her ear against an oak tree
near the mouth of the Kennet River.
I am tired but Catrin takes me by my arm
up to the long barrow on a path winding
between fields of wheat. We stand where over
and over for a thousand years bones were placed
and then taken away. I have read that people
who know they will die in days sing differently
from those who will die in weeks. We know little
of these people whose bones rested here—how they hunted
with yew bows as long as themselves the animals
which were also their gods; or if they stopped
in their running, mouths open, gasping for breath
because of love; or sang in a particular way
close to death every day of their lives.

The Bay Window

More often now I'm slow to look at you,
at the resignation and age chasing death.
I see the plate of your skull
where you have lost your hair.
Tonight I look out the bay window
hoping for the sea but the day
has gone, leaving only black,
a string of orange lights around the promenade,
and your reflection in the glass.
I have no trouble gazing at it
as if you are far away
living in a monk's cell,
sitting at a desk reading,
stroking your beard, the light
on your wrist and one side of your face.
For a moment I am happy,
more at peace with this reflection
than your solid back in a purple shirt
only a body's length from me.

Red Dress

It's summer and I'm wearing my red dress,
lost and helpless under it. Words tonight
not leading me anywhere. I confess:

I mistook the soft rain on the skylight
for your body slowly climbing the stairs
to the high room where I sit and watch bright

leaves turn from green to black, then disappear.
Your equally lost and helpless body,
which was not climbing after all, aware

every sigh moves me away like the sea
tossing a small red boat in its boredom.
Take me to the river close to the trees.

Let me listen to water, the night come
sliding through the weeds. Cover me with praise
and argument among the tall pines. Then come

to me with more than silence, more than noise,
lost and helpless as we are throughout our days.

Haunting and Calling

Halfway across that liminal sea,
I turn my back on the island, a layer of mist
descending upon it, and face inland.
The company of ghosts,
those who are dead and those
who are still alive, can be dangerous,
but I love my ghosts. I love the people
whose ghost I am. In that haunting,
the divine imagination has its way,
though the flesh is denied its place.
I know the body is crying—calling me
even in this time of life. As I was called
out from the manse as a child
to build a raft to float on the waiting water
running through the trespassed property
of the nearby woods.

Living in the Manse

Long afternoon hours stretch into evening
and you are in the high attic trying
to get somewhere else—playing
with a doll's house you must have thought
would someday be your house—
the green sofa and armchairs,
the piece of plastic for the shower,
the little bed you'd sleep in.
Now that dream house lies trashed
on its side in the basement.
Look here. You are not a doll.
Your children are grown.
The small furniture now displayed
on shelves in front of books
where the words of poets strain
after another kind of place—like an abbey
destroyed over and over and built again.
Or a shallow ford in the river
where you can cross to the other side.

Nonresident

It is Midsummer's Eve in a small Russian city.
People are bathing for purification,
stepping over glass in the dirty water.

I walk slower and slower as we drift down the road.
No one notices.
I could wade into the grey river and disappear.

I burned a candle yesterday for love
in the church of Peter and Paul.
I copied what an old woman did.

Lit it and then backed off to let it burn.

Pilgrimage

The sun rises in New England and enters
the window of my study, creating the shadow
of prison bars on my wall and the head of a prisoner.
Light pulsates with the wind in the pines,
and two crosses appear as they do in the sands
near the tip of Llanddwyn in Wales. One in the east
and one in the west. I join the long line
of pilgrims in love, yellow grasses
and furze on either side of the path.
A row of stone cottages waits at the end,
black-backed gulls riding the wind.

Lines

This morning I can't remember my dream,
though I linger in bed. Finally
I open my eyes, defeated,
and look at you, lost in your dream—
perhaps the passion you told me
yesterday you were imagining.
The lines on your forehead
are like the winding paths
made by sheep over the moors.
Maybe you're hitchhiking with me
over those moors in the north of England
towards the stone finials of a Jacobean house.
In a room hangs a painting of the young Milton.
A woman plays a harpsichord before the fire;
we sit on either side of the open hearth.

Marriage

Far away from you I am watching the snow,
the sun on my tilted face and my eyes closed,
the pulsing red under my eyelids like no
red anywhere in this world except for the fields

of war. Fields I have never seen. Fields
I can only imagine. We have traveled long together
like souls arriving each day at the abbey in Wales—
those there either lost or intending to be there—

what was once a center, now an outlying post.
Behind and up the mountain, isolated lakes,
land turned over and strained for shards of the lost,
holy wells entrammeled somewhere in the woods.

We live our time with the known and unknown—
the quivering branch, the bird flown.

Night Watch

Life can ruin something in us
and we live with that ruin
or we live in the ruin
like mountain sheep sheltering
in an abandoned shepherd's hut
looking over the Elan Valley—
beautiful but stricken with bitter rain.
The hut dank with cold when shepherds
once huddled through the dark hours—
as we huddled together last night.
It could have been the end of the world.
Something in me wanted it to be.
But that ruined place has made a prayer
that keeps praying inside me.

III · THE EROTICS OF ABSENCE

First Meditation

Simple words begin it

breaking again. Music is impossible now, that
vibration. And light is too tender, too

bright, too simply falling on the branch.

Making it almost erotic, but
not quite all the way there.

Always I am, in some way

I don't understand, a virgin.
A hunter, like Diana. A tracker. Yes.

What are our lives for? This amazing and simple
breath, this eternal wind that blows,

carrying us in boats over water so vast,
so shimmering in the moonlight,

hoping for a new land, or the old country.

I almost fall asleep in my thinking, almost swoon.
Did the heart begin broken?

Childhood

Sometimes she threatened to send me
to the House of the Good Shepherd
where the orphans lived. One day
I walked out of our small kitchen on Holland Avenue
down Briar to Genesee Street and checked
myself in. Words are enough
to be the cold oatmeal in the morning,
the muffled night silence of children
who have forgotten how to cry.
All I could hear was some kind of shuffling—
as if in their dreams the orphans
were walking somewhere in shoes
that were too large or too small
and belonged to someone else.

Finally

1.

I would never be able to examine
or touch it alive but
it was dead
its body flattened by a quick wheel,
arrested in its final twist,
a fly walking over it while I sit in the dirt
looking at the snake whose body
no longer comes between us.
This most common of snakes
which had, ultimately, to leave itself
to join me on this summer day,
my fingers running over its green back.

2.

Finally I get to kiss you
he said, as I passed
through the reception line after his marriage.
I was just sixteen and didn't
get the full, sad irony
of his words as he bent
his head to mine.
Though I did think of all those
secret meetings in the town library
after school and how sometimes
in the museum, we sat
on marble benches, not touching,
surrounded by paintings,
Thomas Cole promising heaven.

Eternity

In a way we were like them, only
we knew each other for a few years
in the last quarter of the twentieth century
in a small American town. You talked
and I listened as we walked
the back streets near the brick factories.
Weather made no difference. What
was said made no difference. Even now
I can keep us crossing the stone bridge,
staring into the reflecting pool.
Dorothy kept recording in her journals
walks with Coleridge, even on days
he was known to be somewhere else.
So I can keep us on these hard streets—
like the two of them eternally walking
in the north of England, sheltering
from rain under the holly trees.

Wing

I can write nothing
as graceful as the wing
of the dragonfly
resting for a moment
on the corner of this
white page while I rest
for a while
thinking of you.
I wish I could send
something as delicate,
as easily seen through
as this holy lace,
so you would forgive me
everything. Even these
words you would never
want me to write.

City and Lake

Everything in your life
has brought you here
where the mortal city
is erotic even to the red
geraniums on the fire escapes,
the ceiling fan riffling
papers on the table,
finches jumping to perches
and nuzzling in each other's
sides through the dark hours.
Next week at dusk
on the northern lake the sky
locks up its courts. The erotic
changes and acquires depth.
All night the available wind
slaps water against the boat.

The Rains Came

And the lake took into itself
what the heavens had to offer
during a new moon.
The water, this morning,
like a woman full after love
and stunned with serenity.
Wind moves the trees
shaking the last rain down
as a man shudders
in the final moments of his passion.
In secrets we are most ourselves.
How alone I am
sitting by the lake after the rains.

Rembrandt's Women

The curves of the bodies look like mine
and sometimes the color of the hair. So I wonder
what all his sleeping women are dreaming
and where I am amongst the subjects
of temptation, accusation, seduction.
Antiope, Potiphar's wife, Bathsheba.
I don't know what to measure myself by.
I, too, want to sit in front of a window,
close my eyes, and feel the warmth of the sun.
I could stand, like Cleopatra,
and hold my breast, my other hand
firmly around the snake's head.
Instead, I sit alone stripped
to the waist with only the firelight
and the shadows playing about my form.

The Sweater

I walk slowly from one stall
to another, barely looking
at the old clothes and odds
and ends from people's lives.
I feel the desolation,
smell it, do not want to buy
someone else's sadness.
Nevertheless, later I find myself
wearing a black wool sweater
once owned and worn by some
other woman. I am thinking
I might have to give up
being loved. I might
have to give up history—
as simply as I have put on
this sweater, as simply as I sit looking
out the window at the oak tree
shriven by the north wind.

Yew

You break off and keep a small piece
of the tree growing over the poet's grave.
It lies between us in the car.
I want to break it further,
rub the leaves between my fingers
to smell whatever there is
to smell, but I don't.
It is yours. However, the end is
always in the beginning—
the branch is broken from the tree
and will not stay green.
As I sit in thought with my desire,
already it is darkening
and weakening. In the even wind
of eternity, it will not matter
if I break again what is
already broken, enjoy
its perfume for the last time.

Forged

Passion lives also as absence—has an obsession
of its own—insistent, physical.

Nothing escapes it. Ferns leaning towards the rocks
and the rock placed on another rock.

Trees against the sky. A necklace lying
on a woman's neck. The world a world

of copulation. The past entering the present.
The way we can still see a man breathing

after he has died. When will the sound of the bow
drawn over a violin, the vibrato and the tapping of drums,

not take me back to the northern lake
and the water slapping against the boat?

In the Russian Museum

I am in love with Vadim Sidur,
the man who placed this man's boot,
black and worn from war,
against a woman's white
high-heeled shoe, holding
each other up. Sidur is gone
the way of the man and the woman
whose feet shaped this black boot,
this high-heeled shoe,
kissing each other. Enough
to damn war, yes,
but more than enough
to make me jealous of the dead.

In the National Gallery

It is hard to tell if Rembrandt loved
the bodies of women or hated them.
Certainly he was interested.
And how many times have I begun
in love and ended up hating
the continual subject, for it gives
the impression I can't
grow up, can't move on.
His one dead woman hanging
from a gibbet drew my attention
more than all the other live
beauties, naked or bedecked.
Here is the final spectacle—the dead
weight of the dangling limbs
pulled only by gravity. Here, finally,
a body with no desire.

Second World

Although I had been instructed not to arrive
sooner than five hours after the ECT treatment,
they unlocked the door of the ward. As I
turned the corner I saw my mother walking,
her head lowered, a nurse holding her arm.
When she saw me, she began to cry.
I am so alone, she said. For a moment
I glimpsed the grey, barren plains
she was still walking, alone and unattended,
sorting the great foundations of her being.
That was the beginning of my hours,
days and evenings, on the ward as a visitor.
After dinner I would sit in the lounge as if
I were one of them—playing cards, watching
old videos. No one was leaving. We
are stopped from being with those we love
at the worst times, and we acquiesce.
In turn, giving up any hope that someone
will walk back from hell with us.
I loved that ward, felt more comfortable
there than almost anywhere.
The men and women expected nothing
and everything—like those on Noah's ark,
surrounded by water for forty days and nights.
They were all there was of the lost news
from the old world. Some of them
would see the great mountains of Ararat.

Forgotten

You signed out of the hospital's ward
that winter afternoon. There was nothing
to do but breathe the air of an unfamiliar town
in bitter cold, entering discount stores for warmth:
a mother and daughter together.
No one noticed your blue coat, my red hair,
our controlled silence and quiet talk
as we crossed and recrossed the white streets,
trying to keep you in this world.
You have forgotten all of this—
what you wore, the cheap clothing stores,
even why we were there. I can't tell the difference
between love and attachment any more.
We held each other's familiar arms as we walked
the streets of a small town near a frozen lake.

IV · MONEY FOR THE BOATMAN

Let my pen grow wet with tears for its theme is grief,
Let it not lack beauty, let not the letters cease.

Latin verse lament

Winter

I call my mother on the phone and we sit in silence
as she listens to the nurses' conversations.
I could be calling her in heaven
where she prefers to listen to angels talking
while they wheel the others in, taking off heavy coats,
welcoming them. She knows I am somewhere
down on earth holding a phone and straining after her.
Distance grows between us.
The voices must be listened to—
her business now—how to survive in heaven.

To a Nereid

Do not come yet to escort her. Not yet.
Do not arrive with a water bird under your feet
wet with sea spray. Not yet.

Stopping you drives me out of bed,
insisting I will talk to her today.

I am still reclining in her lap,
wheelchair-ridden as it is.

I am not ready for her not
to arrive again, for me not
to arrive at her door.

I breathe more slowly trying to delay
your inevitable journey over the faraway waves.

Nymph,
I say, not yet: stay standing
between the columns of the tombs.

Desire

The last people on earth don't
touch each other. They barely
want to walk side by side. The air
moves and hurts them. Let's say

the day is one of earth's
lovely and waning days,
sun shining through leaves,
birds heard and almost heard.

On such a day someone pushes my mother
down the hall on a gurney toward me.
She lifts her arm in triumph, in greeting.
She saw my hair, she said. Every part of the body

is heartbreaking. Her shoulder,
my hair. We touch less
and less. We can't stand it,
the slack skin under the arms.

The dead on the fields of war
touch each other this way and that—
head on a knee, arm across a chest,
face on another face. The cold dead,
the sinless dead, touching effortlessly.

And here I am straining with attention,
recoiling, fleeing in place.

Residue

She knows there is somewhere
she wishes to return, but can't
remember where somewhere is.
Pontrhydyfen? Port Talbot?
Not Liverpool in the war.
Aberystwyth? Moriah Church?
Regency Road, Holland Avenue,
Utica, New York. All names
gone. And the roads, sea spray,
promenade, hymn singing,
laughter in the choir's changing room.
Easter lilies, delicate pink
sweet peas in spring, clothes
on the line in summer. Now
home reduced to a shared room
with a stranger—whose name
she can never remember,
this-person-who-has-come-to-
live-in-my-home. (*Home, I guess*
you could call it that, she says.)
I don't belong here; this is
not my room. I enter
the deception: *yes, look*
at the photographs, look
at your beautiful dresser.
Hovering into night,
slowly becoming dead,
she will never be home again.

Passing

The unspoken word is *God*.
It has come to this.

We've all changed; we're all
something else now.

My mother has no idea
where home is; it is *not here*.

The gods need mortal help.
If we don't know the way,

they can do nothing.
This is what it feels like.

The gods pass us by
on the way to somewhere else.

Final Room

What is palpable, what is
invisible? Is the door

she asks me to open the real door
(but it is already open)

or a door to somewhere else?
Is *come with me* an invitation

to the land of the dead? My mind
goes there. I am almost walking there.

I want that invitation. Just to be asked
lends magnitude to the stale odor of flesh,

the beaten dresser and mirror,
the shared room with all she has

in the world. How is it
the absence of God makes God

more present? Or makes me
more present. I think of the words

I read in an old letter protesting
the drowning of a valley in Wales:

I, for one, will be there.

Instruction

Sing to my mother on her boat as it leaves the shore
ringed with the spent purple of lady's-thumb
and vines circling on nothing—only the air
that sustains us all. Everything now has happened.

Winter is coming. And she is leaving slowly.
There is a sleep inside her that has no end.
Truth stands still. Touch her softly.
Murmur low of early violets and the mountain,

of harbors, hidden lanes, stone fences.
Sing of brilliance and the drumming dead,
long walks on the berm of the western seas,
her head thrown back, dress swinging to her stride.

The Welsh miners walked out of the earth singing.
As her boat angles through the long weeds, sing.

Almost Gone

The sky chooses grey in its withdrawal
and you hold back your love. Of course.
Why love while the concert of small snow
is singing a requiem? Near the branch
of the Utley River a truck swallows up
a few words of my prayer. *Forgive us
our sins*...while the broken logs at the edge
of the woods fall into the intimacy of
other trees. I want to fall
into your bones, your thin and old flesh,
the lichen of your eyes. *Pass on, pass on,*
is what you repeat today. And I think
of passion, of the passion of these
moments with you, which lessen
what I had thought passion meant before.
There is no panting, no peak,
just the pinnacle of an edge kept over
and over, a border beyond which
there is an infinite country, or an infinite
backside of the unknown. I am not
thinking that angels and principalities
wait for you, though that image occurs.
Returning from the dead, you ask,
why do they take everything away from me?
The *they* is suddenly palpable. Something
is waiting to take everything away—all that has
no more use, including me. I have
to know this. Including me.

Mair/Mary

Change me, she says.
As if all my life I have not
been trying to do just that. And now

with the animal in the room
breathing its utter demand,
she is still asking. But what change

other than dissolution is possible
now? The urge of the world
does not pass. She is still afraid.

The first words out of the angel's mouth were
Do not be afraid. I am not an angel,
and never wanted to be one, but I want

to believe enough to tell my mother
she has nothing to fear, and later
to have the strength to stand

while she is carried, altered and finished,
through the early morning light.

Early March

You've let us go.
One side of the branch is white

and will be whiter by the end of the day.
The snow is quiet—guileless and tender.

Trees near and in the distance.

Believe me: all cries
are tangled there.

Every cry in the world.
You've let us go

and that is the way
I will walk now.

The Other Side of Waiting

We know from the old stories that death is a god,
but not the god who spits into our mouths.

He has rescued me. Each time my mother came back
from the dead, she was more spirit than body.

One word came out of her mouth—the mouth
I learned to kiss again.

Death is the god who shows us the other side of waiting.
He was waiting and I was waiting.

We held our breath watching her breath.

What did it take for him to wave his cloak
between us for the final time?

Worlds

The other world I once lived in
had my mother in it. The drumming
of the earth was loud in the final days,
and there was always a demand
or an invitation: cross the long bridge
over the Hudson River, bend my head
over her, in the smallest room let her go.
All rigorous and rewarding. Before evening
birds sent their cries toward the sky
while the sun grew tired of burning
and disappeared. In that other world
there was a first home in a body
reduced at the end to bone and bent fingers.
But a home, nevertheless.

Money for the Boatman

I did not get to press the coins into her hand,
arriving after it was over.

Driving home that evening,
the sentinels of the tall grasses
seemed to turn their heads away.

Today I take the long road back.
Red tulips in the trunk of the car,
color draining out of them.

I travel towards a grave,
a stone, a view of the hills
circling the Mohawk Valley.

I travel for intimacy with the dead.

What does this say
about my life, the loves
in my life? Are we

always moving towards
some earlier and earlier
claim that history has over us—

that nothing in the present or the future
can compare to? And now,

the earlier claim
is in the spirit world,

which means it is permanent.

73

Final Position

I believe you kept on living
so that you could stay here with me.
You had used yourself completely up;

there could have been no other reason.
And you wanted me to go with you,
as if you didn't care it meant

I would have to die too. I think
I have gone to find you. I am walking
behind you on the other side of the hedge,

and the longer I do this the larger everything becomes.
But I can walk only so far as the earth allows.
Eternity is all I care about now—the eternity

in which you are walking with a body
no longer in that final position
lying underneath a sheet.

After

While I am here on earth
you will not be

like some long-lost possession
for which one no longer looks.

But where now?

I begin in the ways
I afflict myself.

And then in the ways
of laughter and clamor.

And always along the roads,
in the birch woods,
the snow sharp against my face.

It seems there is no rousing you.
Life waits. Life waits.

The raft I dreamt of as a child
was never built, though even now
I think of it. But what was fashioned

to deliver me here on this shore?
On this shore where living is like building

a house from stones of the old court
where bards once were singing.

V · UNDER A SKY

Pretending on the Backwaters

I took a pleasure ride with friends
on the backwaters of the Arabian Sea,
feigned interest in the fishing nets
and water-crows shining in the sun.
Over time the moon rose in the sky.

One by one people left my company
so that finally, in the boat's prow,
I sat alone pretending. Pretending
I was not arriving where I find myself now—
on another continent at the end of winter,

at the end of a dream, and knowing
it doesn't matter that around the bend
of the frozen lake is an old summer.
It just doesn't matter that the gods
are dancing somewhere deep in stone.

Not About Daily Life

It is not anonymity I want anymore,
but a strict silence
in which something can be understood.
This is not about daily life.
I am capable of that.
But during the day I dream
of wanting my head cut off and held,
the heaviness draining and words
flowing away. The colors are black and red.
The moment, classical.
I wait for this, preparing to live in a palace,
putting perfume on my feet
in case I find myself walking there.

Candle for the Dead

FOR GARETH

It is a rainy and grey day.
The graveyard at the end
of the street stands still.
I rush home from work to watch
the candle's last flickering struggle
and sit on the far side of the room.
The sound of the world is not
too far away. All over the city
people are making plans. Finally
I squat near the edge of the low table,
look down at the candle burning
in a small clear sea, and catch the light's
final glance—not like
my brother's stricken face
propped in the white hospital bed.
Gone somewhere. Gone on an old
train winding up the valleys.
Going and stopping. Going
and stopping.

Company

Blue irises open one by one. The heavy
wooden chairs on the patio
placed as if all night the dead
had sat and spoken of us.
They wore large black woolen coats
because the wind was cold,
the moon behind clouds.
They knew I was tossing and turning,
that I had taken a pill to help me sleep—
wanting a little death. They talked
and laughed softly, now and then.
Not speaking of anything
we would think of as important.
The ferns are bruised this morning
where coats had brushed against them.

Angels

Why do I cry at the thought of you?
Are you my dead father preaching
from Moriah's pulpit? Or my dead brother,
the one I sat with through the early years
in the second row of the small congregation?
I try every night, like Isis, to piece him together.
Or are you my son I cannot shield from pain?
My love, finally, only the love of a mother.
Sometimes I think you are one of the three
strange angels standing at my door—knocking
and knocking—unable to leave me alone.

Untitled

She is listening to the wood burning
and also looking out the window
where the snow is deep and the wind
lifts the few solitary leaves remaining.
The fire is not her passion and the drifting snow
not loneliness. The flayed and clinging
leaves are not her need; nor the sudden blizzard
confusion. The shadow under the tree is not
her dying mother, or an emblem of her own death.
All is unaccountable and ancient.
The triumph of rushes in the thigh-high snow
is not triumph. The small flakes drifting
by the white birch are not the invisible world.
The receding pine trees, not distance;
certainly not dispensation.

Far from Shore

My body is a boat owned
by the olive green sand
at the bottom of the river
in late winter. Owned
by the rain raining
on an ocean whose sun
no one sees. The water
entering the water over and over.
Impossibly deep and far away.

Uncertainties, Mysteries

Between Welsh and English there is silence,
a door facing two ways.
Do I go north? Across water?
Over land? Through memory?
What lies between *coeden* and *tree*?
Môr and *sea*? *Nos* and *night*? A hesitation.
A choice. I say *afon* and I'm walking
in mid Wales or I think of a mouth;
I think of a gift. If I say *river*, I'm praying
over a bridge; I'm writing a letter.
Morning I wake in my own bed;
Bore the sun rises near a harbor.
I say *llyn* and think of my father;
lake, my childhood, my children.
If I say *cariad* I remember Gareth and his death;
I say *love* and think of failure and the mysteries.

The Other Music in Her Throat

She remembers with longing
the children dancing in *Black Orpheus*
as the music slowly lifts the red sun
out of the southern sea.
But because when she sings,
she can hear another voice singing
in her throat, she stops
and simply listens to the others
as they carry the tune,
though not as well as she could—
a girl brought up in congregations
breaking out in four-part harmony.
But now there is this other music
in her throat forever.
Then the large silence she makes
when she stops to stop
that second voice from singing.

Early October

Something is trying to come through
in the familiar yard
with the white metal table rusting,
the birdhouse lying on its side in the grass.
The spider's long threads shine floating
in the air and cling to the tomato stalks.
Everything moves slightly
in the fall morning.
Something is trying to come through
in the still and waiting yard,
while under her shirt an old world
has not quite given up.

Posing for Rembrandt

Posing, I cling to a rope strung
from the high bedpost. Later
my raised right hand will hold an arrow.
My body strung this way
to reveal the underside
of arm and its dark pit,
the stretch of breasts, twist
of waist, light breaking
over my soft stomach,
the line of my buttocks.
Venus this time,
handing the arrow to Cupid?
Or Diana before her secret pool
with Actaeon's eyes upon her
like Rembrandt's on my body,
minutely observing to inform
the world. Of course later
he will leave out the rope
I cling to for hours
until it becomes home,
cling to so long I feel my weight
stretched taut and then my bones,
thinner and thinner, until I become
the first ray of light breaking out of night.

In the Presence of the Lord

I'm walking towards the crossroads and may arrive
tomorrow. Meanwhile my feet worry the dirt
with purpose. This is one way to be alive.
But at the crossroads, the dead are buried—the wretched,

unknown dead who travelled as far as they could
and then were done. Some were carried, some
carried themselves. There the noise of the world
stops. The stamping heart separates from the dumb,

tired, finished body. I sigh and whisper—
walk towards the crossroads while the winter trees
divide against the sky, the stones endure,
birds watch with their cold black eyes.

This is how to be alive and not undone.
Carry sound as long and as far as you can.

Liturgy

Our hearts are like the red bell tolling
in the ocean, ringing and tolling,
tossed by waves and pushed by the wind,
as we pass by in a boat on the way to the far island.

Let me remember sailing boats made of grass
while my father preached of the Resurrection
in a nearby country church. Now and then
I could hear the singing of hymns.

Walking with Natalya

There cannot be an argument with death—
holly and black raspberry bushes
grow over the slate gravestones.

In the old tales, soldiers ride the swift horses
which later wander without riders
in the gleaming forest.

I am sorry, I want to say to her:
today my heart is full of grief.

Instead I point out lupine, foxglove,
a blackbird biting a worm in two,
a grey dove against the grey sky.

I wonder if these flowers and birds
live in her city in the Ural Mountains.

She tells me of the wild tribesmen
in the snow deserts of the north
who sing about whatever they happen to see.

They sing with joy, she says,
without thought, without intention.

Under a Sky

Three people are walking
down a road. Sometimes
their backs are to me,

sometimes I am one of them.
I would like to be always
one of the three walking

down a road under a sky.
I wouldn't care about talk
or need to know our destination.

For days our stride would be long
and one of us would swing her arms.
We'd see stone and cattails along the edges.

Later, wild roses and ferns.
After a while we would not
remember where we came from

and would not be thinking of arrival.
Even in the winter months
we'd be walking, moving always.

Past cities and ruined farms. Past
stands of birch and the sea.

Finished and Waiting

Again, the day is almost perfect. The world
cannot be faulted. There are still
embers underneath the ash—
men, women, and children curled in their cloaks,
exhausted from the feasting and revelry.
There was no right choice for Paris—
only different tales told throughout the night.
Everything is finished and also waiting. Now
it is mid-August in another century.
The cows of heaven are not grazing on earth.
But I am thinking of them,
I see them moving slowly
in the dew-soaked field next to the woods.

NOTES

The five paintings in the book are watercolors by Margaret Lloyd. Of these the first four are held in private collections:

Part I: *The Sea is Rough*
Part II: *Trees*
Part III: *Transfiguration*
Part IV: *Night's Estate*
Part V: *Standing Stones*

Several poems are connected to works of art:

"Ariadne": *Ariadne*, John Lavery
"Annunciation": icon in Pskov, Russia
"Sebastian": *Saint Sebastian*, Andrea Mantegna
"Raised": *Christ at the Sea of Galilee*, Jacopo Tintoretto
"In David's City": *Bathsheba with King David's Letter*, Rembrandt van Rijn
"In the Russian Museum": sculpture, Vadim Sidur
"In the National Gallery": *A Woman Hanging on a Gibbet, 1664*, Rembrandt van Rijn
"Posing for Rembrandt": *A Woman with an Arrow*, Rembrandt van Rijn

I OWE A GREAT DEBT to the living and to the dead. Past and present members of Group 18, a poetry workshop centered in Northampton, Massachusetts, have been my mainstay and lifeline as a poet. Particular thanks to Henry Lyman, David Lloyd, Annie Woodhull, Bill O'Connell, and Roz Driscoll, all of whom read and commented on the book in manuscript form. I am very grateful to Gordon Thorne and Open Field Press for publishing *Forged Light*. Michael Russem made this book elegant and beautiful; Steve Strimer and Collective Copies made it real. The great and fine spirits of my two children, Bryn and Catrin Lloyd-Bollard, continue as beacons. I am always and forever obligated to John Bollard, who has lent unceasing, intelligent, and spirited support to my creative life.

MARGARET LLOYD was born in Liverpool, England, of Welsh parents and grew up in a Welsh community in central New York state. Fairleigh Dickinson University Press published *William Carlos Williams' Paterson: A Critical Reappraisal*, now considered seminal in the field. Alice James Books brought out her first book of poems, *This Particular Earthly Scene*. Plinth Books published Lloyd's second collection of poems, *A Moment in the Field: Voices from Arthurian Legend*. Her poetry honors include a National Endowment for the Humanities grant, fellowships to the Bread Loaf Writers Conference and to Hawthornden Castle in Scotland, and a writing residency at Yaddo, where she worked on the poems in *Forged Light*. A poet and painter, Lloyd is Professor of English and Chair of the Humanities Department at Springfield College.